MEXICO

A TRUE BOOK

by

Ann Heinrichs

Children's Press®

A Division of Grolier Publishing

New York London Hong Kong Sydney
Danbury, Connecticut

Reading Consultant
Linda Cornwell
Learning Resource Consultant
Indiana Department of
Education

A Mexican girl

Library of Congress Cataloging-in-Publication Data

Heinrichs, Ann.
   Mexico / by Ann Heinrichs.
     p. cm. — (A true book)
   Includes index.
   ISBN 0-516-20337-1(lib. bdg.)   0-516-26173-8 (pbk.)
   1. Mexico—Juvenile literature. I. Title. II. Series.
F1208.5.H45 1997
972—dc20   96-28156
                                        CIP
                                        AC

Contents

UNITED STATES

Caribbean Sea

BELIZE
GUATEMALA

Gulf of Mexico

Yucatán Peninsula

0   200 miles

0   300 kilometers

N
W   E
S

• Monterrey

EASTERN SIERRA MADRE

MEXICO

Rio Grande

Mexico City ★

• Puebla

Guadalajara •

WESTERN SIERRA MADRE

Gulf of California

Baja California

PACIFIC OCEAN

MEXICO

Mountains and Mesas

Mexico is the northernmost country in Latin America. It lies directly south of the United States. Mexico borders the Pacific Ocean on the west. Its east coast faces the Gulf of Mexico and the Caribbean Sea.

Mexico shares its northern border with the U.S. states of

Texas, New Mexico, Arizona, and California. The Rio Grande (Spanish for "Big River") forms much of this border. At Mexico's northwest tip is a long, narrow peninsula called Baja California, which means "Lower California."

At the southern end of Mexico lies the Yucatán Peninsula. Guatemala and Belize are Mexico's southern neighbors. Jungles and rain forests cover much of the

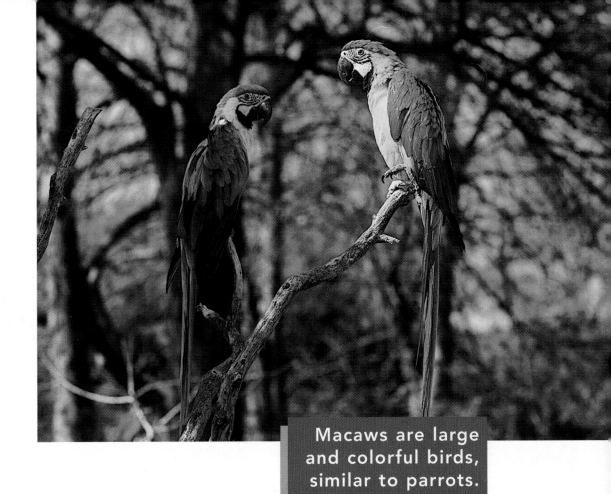

Macaws are large and colorful birds, similar to parrots.

southern part of the country. The wildlife of Mexico includes monkeys, parrots, and macaws.

The landscape of Mexico varies from dry deserts (left) to high mountains (above).

Most of Mexico is made up of a high mesa, or plateau. In the north, the mesa is rough and dry, with deserts and rocky mountains. Rattlesnakes, prairie dogs, coyotes, and mountain lions make their homes there. Many of Mexico's largest cities lie farther south.

Mountain ranges called the eastern and western Sierra Madres run north and south through Mexico. The western Sierra Madres are so rugged and wild that some areas have never been explored.

People of Many Cultures

Mexico is home to about 94 million people—more people than any other Spanish-speaking country in the world. Today, most Mexicans are descendants of both Indian and Spanish people. They are proud of their culture and do not think of themselves as either Spanish or Indian. Instead, they are a special blend

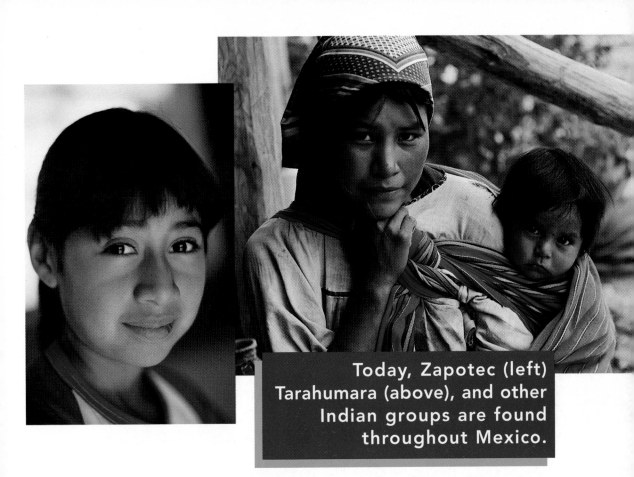

Today, Zapotec (left) Tarahumara (above), and other Indian groups are found throughout Mexico.

of both. Some Mexicans are descendants of only Spanish or other European people.

Mexico's Indians have an ancient cultural heritage. Their ancestors include Maya,

Aztec, Zapotec, Yaqui, and Tarahumara people.

Spanish is Mexico's major language. It is a little different from the Spanish that is spoken in Spain. Indians speak the languages of their ancestors. Mexicans usually have two family names. After a person's first and middle names come the father's last name, then the mother's.

Most Mexicans practice the Roman Catholic religion. Many combine Indian customs with Catholicism.

Mexico City is the capital of Mexico.

About seven of ten Mexicans live in cities. Mexico City is the capital of Mexico. It is also the largest city in Mexico. More than 20 million people live there. Other large cities include Guadalajara, Monterrey, and Puebla.

Early Empires

The ancient Olmec people lived along Mexico's east coast from about 800 B.C. to A.D. 250. The Olmecs were expert scientists and artists. By studying the sun and stars, they made a calendar.

The Maya lived in southern Mexico between 300 B.C. and A.D. 900. They built huge stone pyramids with temples at the top. The

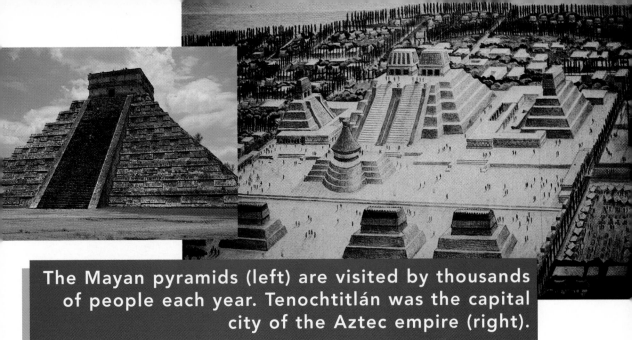

The Mayan pyramids (left) are visited by thousands of people each year. Tenochtitlán was the capital city of the Aztec empire (right).

Maya also developed a writing system that used pictures and symbols, instead of letters.

The Aztecs arrived in central Mexico around A.D. 1200. Over time, they built a vast empire. Their capital was Tenochtitlán. Its central plaza is now Mexico City's Zócalo Plaza.

The Spanish Conquest

The Italian explorer Christopher Columbus sailed across the Atlantic Ocean from Spain in 1492. He landed on an island only a few hundred miles from Mexico. Columbus thought he had reached the Indies in Asia, so he called the people living in the region "Indians."

Christopher Columbus (left) and Hernando Cortés (right)

Soon after, Spanish explorers set sail for Mexico. They were called conquistadores, or conquerors. One of these conquistadores was Hernando Cortés. He and his army invaded the Aztec capital of Tenochtitlán in 1519.

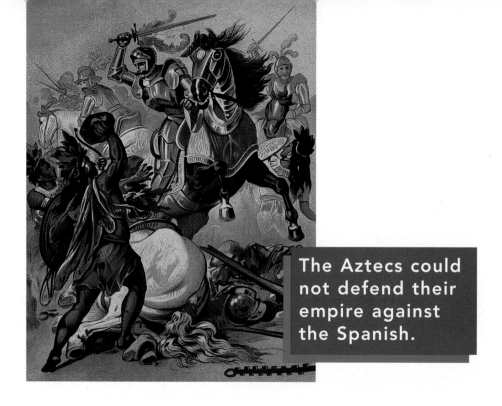

The Aztecs could not defend their empire against the Spanish.

The Aztecs had no defenses against the Spaniards' guns and cannons. The Aztecs had never before seen horses, which the Spaniards were riding. In 1521, the Aztec empire fell to Cortés and the Spaniards.

Mexico became a Spanish colony. Governors came from Spain to rule. Spanish missionaries arrived too. They taught the Roman Catholic religion to the Indians and built churches and schools. Many churches that were built during the time of Spanish rule are still standing in Mexico.

This cathedral in Mexico City was built in 1667.

Mexican Pyramids

Religion was very important to the early Indians of Mexico. Many Indian groups built pyramids with steps that led to the top. Some of the pyramids were 210 feet (64 meters) high. At the top of the pyramids were temples that were used for religious ceremonies.

Thousands of people each year travel to Mexico to see the ruins of the ancient pyramids.

Independence

Eventually, Mexico's Indians revolted against Spanish rule. In 1810, a priest named Miguel Hidalgo y Costilla called for a rebellion to free Mexico from Spain. Mexico's war for independence began soon after. Finally, in 1821, Mexico won its freedom.

Miguel Hidalgo y Costilla

At that time, Mexico was much larger than it is today. Its border extended into the present-day states of Texas, Utah, Nevada, and California. Most of New Mexico, Arizona, and Colorado were also part of Mexico.

Texas fought Mexico for its own independence, and won in 1836. Then the United States and Mexico went to war from 1846 to 1848. Mexico lost. The United States paid $15 million to Mexico, which gave up two-fifths of its territory to the United States.

Benito Juárez

Benito Juárez, a Zapotec Indian, became president of Mexico in 1858. He divided up many large estates to give poor Mexicans more land.

Another president, Porfirio Díaz, ruled as a dictator. In 1910, Mexicans rebelled against him in a revolution that lasted until 1920. After the second revolution, land was again distributed more fairly. Many schools were built, and living conditions improved.

Today, Mexico's leaders face problems of unemployment, high prices, pollution, and drugs. They are working hard to improve life for all Mexicans.

How People Live

In large cities, Mexicans dress similarly to people in United States or European cities. They live in modern apartment buildings or houses. Homes in the wealthier areas are large and beautifully decorated. In city slums, though, poor people live in

Some of the homes in Mexico are very large (left). Adobe homes (right) are made of sun-dried clay.

shacks made of cardboard or metal. Homes made of white adobe (sun-dried clay) with red tile roofs can be found throughout Mexico. In some regions, homes are made of wooden poles with thatched roofs.

The streets of Mexico City are jammed with traffic, but life is much quieter in small villages. People carry goods to market on burros (small donkeys), in carts, or in baskets on their heads.

This woman sells her roses in an outdoor market.

Food in Mexico is very spicy. Mexicans enjoy eating corn, beans, tomatoes, and peppers. Vegetables, meat, or cheese are often wrapped in thin, flat breads called tortillas. Most

Tortillas are a basic food in Mexico.

Mexicans eat their main meal of the day at around two o'clock in the afternoon.

Fútbol, or soccer, is the most popular sport in Mexico. Rodeos, bullfights, and baseball are favorites too. Mexicans also enjoy strolling in city plazas and listening to live music.

Economy and Jobs

Many people from the country-side move to the cities hoping to find work in hotels, restaurants, or factories. Mexico's factories make chemicals, clothes, steel, cars, and car parts. About half of all the country's factories are in the Mexico City area. Other factories, built along Mexico's

An automobile factory near Mexico City

northern border, make goods for companies in the United States.

Much of Mexico's wealth still lies underground. Silver, sulfur, lead, zinc, and gold mines are found throughout the country.

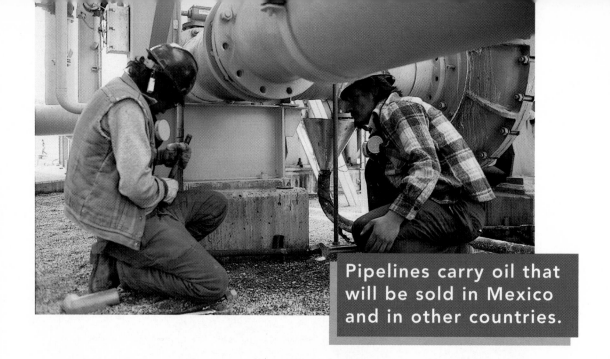

Pipelines carry oil that will be sold in Mexico and in other countries.

In 1900, oil was discovered on the east coast of Mexico. Today, Mexico is one of the world's most important oil-producing countries.

Many Mexicans are farm-workers. Crops thrive in the rich soil of southern Mexico,

Many Mexican farmers use horses for farming instead of machinery.

while land in the north is better for grazing cattle.

Corn is Mexico's major crop. Mexican farmers also raise beans, coffee, cotton, wheat, bananas, and vanilla. Another important crop is cacao, which is used to make chocolate.

A truck carries goods across the U.S.–Mexican border. NAFTA made it easier for Mexico to do business with the United States and Canada.

In 1994, a trade agreement with the United States and Canada went into effect. It was called the North American Free Trade Agreement (NAFTA). This agreement made it easier and less expensive for Mexico to trade goods with its North American neighbors.

Fiestas, Music, and Arts

Festivals, called fiestas, are fun and exciting events in Mexico. The people celebrate with fireworks, music, dancing, and a lot of food.

At Christmastime, children have fun breaking piñatas. A piñata is a papier-mâché animal stuffed with candy, fruit, and toys.

Breaking a piñata is a popular fiesta activity for children.

It is hung up above the children's heads. Wearing a blindfold, the children try to break the piñata open with a long stick. When the piñata breaks, the treats come falling out.

Each December 12, Mexicans honor the Virgin of Guadalupe, Mexico's patron saint. Other important holidays are Independence Day (September 16) and the Day of the Dead (November 2).

Children prepare to celebrate the Virgin of Guadalupe festival, held each year on December 12.

The Day of the Dead

In Spanish, the Day of the Dead is called *El Día de los Muertos*. It is a happy festival that honors friends and family members who have died. Many children dress up in costumes and masks. They also receive candy, and they parade through the streets.

Families visit the graves of their loved ones. They bring flowers and light candles. Many families have picnics at the gravesite and eat some of the favorite foods of their loved one.

Mexican artists are well known for their beautiful crafts.

Mexican artists are known for their murals, or wall paintings. Murals by Diego Rivera and José Orozco tell stories of the Mexican revolution. Mexican artists also make pottery, silver jewelry, and hand-woven cloth.

Music is an important part of Mexico's culture. Mariachi musicians in their huge *charro* hats stroll through cafés playing guitars, trumpets, and violins. Folk dancers wear dazzling costumes as they twirl and tap their feet. The lively rhythms capture the spirit of Mexico's proud heritage. Folk songs called *corridos* tell of the heroes who helped shape Mexico's colorful past.

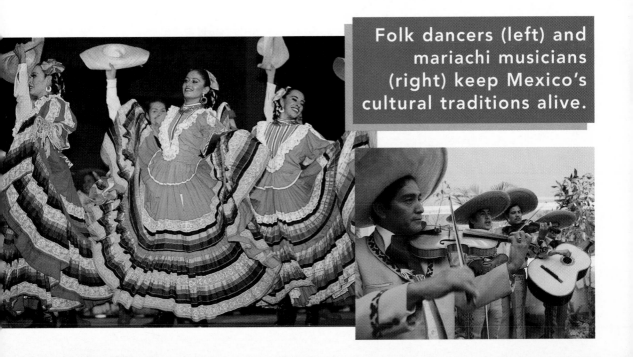

Folk dancers (left) and mariachi musicians (right) keep Mexico's cultural traditions alive.

To Find Out More

Here are some additional resources to help you learn more about the nation of Mexico:

 **Books**

 **Organizations**

Franco, Betsy. **Around the World, Vol 1: Mexico.** Evan-Moor Corp., 1993.

Parker, Lewis. **Dropping in on Mexico.** Rourke Book Co., 1994.

Silverthorne, Elizabeth. **Fiesta: Mexico's Great Celebrations.** Millbrook Press, 1992.

Wolf, Bernard. **Beneath the Stone: A Mexican Zapotec Tale.** Orchard Books, 1994.

Center for U.S. Mexican Studies
c/o University of California
La Jolla, California 92093

Mexican American Cultural Center
3019 W. French Place
San Antonio, Texas 78228

Mexican Tourism Office
1911 Pennsylvania Ave., NW
Washington, D.C. 20006

Mexico: Fiestas and Events

http://mexico-travel.com/fiestas/fiestas.html

Learn all about national, state, and regional festivals, including the Mole Fair, Radish Night, the Sherbet Fair, and many other Mexican holiday celebrations.

Planet Earth Home Page: Country of Mexico

http://nosc.mil/planet_earth/countries/mexico.html

Visit Mexican cities, view maps, get facts and figures, and learn about culture and society in modern Mexico.

World of the Mayas

http://bertha.pomona.claremont.edu.cslo/mcushman/final.html

Discover the art, science, history, and culture of the Maya.

See What's New in Mexico

http://gaia.ecs.csus.edu/~arellano/index.html

See Mexican paintings and photographs, learn about art history, read a magazine or newspaper, drop in on a radio station, get information about Mexico City and other fun places, and visit the home pages of Mexican soccer teams.

Important Words

ancestors relatives who lived a long time ago

colony territory ruled by another country

economy a country's wealth, based the goods and services it produces

heritage customs, history, and arts from a country's past

Latin America Mexico, Central America, and South America

patron saint saint who is celebrated as the special protector of a country

peninsula land surrounded by water on three sides

plaza public square in the center of a city

Index

Meet the Author

Ann Heinrichs grew up in Arkansas and lives in Chicago, Illinois. She has written more than twenty books about American, Asian, and African history and culture. She has also written numerous newspaper, magazine, and encyclopedia articles.

Besides the United States, she has traveled in Europe, North Africa, the Middle East, and east Asia. The desert is her favorite terrain.

Other True Books by Ann Heinrichs about countries of the world include *Brazil*, *China*, *Japan*, *South Africa*, and *Venezuela*.

Ms. Heinrichs holds bachelor's and master's degrees in piano performance. For relaxation, she practices chi gung and t'ai chi.